Sojourner Songs

The voice I hear this passing night was heard
In ancient days by emperor and clown:
Perhaps the self-same song that found a path
Through the sad heart of Ruth, when, sick for home,
She stood in tears amid the alien corn.

–from "Ode to a Nightingale"
by John Keats

Praise For
A Small Cup of Light

"Ben Palpant tells his story so very well, weaving past and present, imagination and experience into an amazing tapestry. I was quite taken with it. Honestly, a stunning book. It reminds me of Simone Weil's essay on affliction. Ben has done what few authors do. He has written a book about his own experience of suffering, which was mysterious and tumultuous. Yet he told his story so transparently and effortlessly that I gazed through his story to think about my story and the human story. He also wrote with elegance and grace. It is a superb book in every way."

–Gerald Sittser, professor of Theology at Whitworth University
and author of *A Grace Disguised* and *A Grace Revealed*

"I devoured it. More aptly, I drank it up. It came to me as a purely unexpected gift...smack into a heart of darkness period for me. I gave up underlining because the entire book was being smote by my pen. Every sentence shone. I will say with all honesty that it is one of the best I have ever read. It is a balm and a lamp. It is special. It is pure Holy Spirit gift, giving me the words to give my daughter when she sat up coughing with pneumonia-haunted lungs just last week. Thank you for making me unafraid of suffering. Thank you for passing me God's peace. Thank you for making me ask God to teach me what it is He would have me learn in this season. To sit with and seek why I have been entrusted with this pain.

–Carolyn Weber, author of *Surprised By Oxford* and *Holy Is The Day*

"Ben Palpant is a fellow traveler on the journey through pain and adversity. As such, he knows there are no easy answers or quick fixes when we encounter hardships and heartaches in our lives. With grace and compassion, Ben encourages readers to seek God's presence, even when He seems absent, and pursue transformation, even when it seems impossible. Ben's book arrived in my hands at a time when my well-constructed world was slowly being dismantled. His words, full of warmth and wisdom, provided genuine comfort while challenging me to look squarely at painful issues I'd prefer to avoid. Ben speaks from the heart–and his hard-won insights touched my own. I have read each page slowly and intentionally, and I have been ministered to by Ben's insights, sensitivity, openness, and artistry. Already his book is having a profound influence... certainly on me."

–Keith Wall, coauthor of *Heaven and the Afterlife*
and *Real Life, Real Miracles*

"In a gorgeous and tender, beautiful and graceful clarion call to the heart of our despair and the fierceness of our inner desolations, Ben Palpant draws us to an intimate encounter with the God of all consolation. He courageously broaches the inner life of weakness and the sorrows we harbor. *A Small Cup of Light* is the sustenance we need to pass through the valley of the shadow and arrive on the other side more whole, more humble, and more alive."

–Shann Ray Ferch, author of *American Masculine* and
Balefire: Poems.

"Adversity, sorrow, disappointment. None of us ever want it. But all of us will surely face it. And when we do, we are invariably surprised, unprepared. Ben Palpant's beautiful book–beautifully conceived and beautifully written–explores the dark profiles of suffering with the glistening light of hope. Reading *A Small Cup of Light* powerfully moved me, not only by reminding me of God's good providence, but also by provoking in me memories of all the ways His providence has sustained me through my own days of bewildering adversities. By all means, *tolle lege*, take and read."

–George Grant, pastor, author, and renowned speaker

"Ben Palpant's *A Small Cup of Light* caused me to weep for joy, opened my mind to dream of future glory, and engaged my heart with gripping stories of personal, searing truth. In these pages, you will find a faithful and honest pilgrim who invites you through deep valleys of pain to illuminate your own mysterious journey with God in surprising joy. If you are like me, you too will find your soul in celebration."

–Dave Hutchins, author of *Courageous Parenting: the passionate pursuit of your teen's heart*

"This is simply a superb book. It is beautifully written, theologically rigorous, elegantly typeset, and carefully designed. Every page was easy to look at and equally easy to turn. This is a book for anyone dealing with (apparently) inexplicable suffering. That may be you, or it may be someone close to you. In this book, Ben Palpant raises all the hard questions without flinching, and offers clear and careful answers that go all the way down to the right part of the soul. He does this without patronizing anybody, or patting the back of the reader's hand once. I know that many would be encouraged by this book, and want to urge them to it. The Puritans were great on the subject of affliction, and here in this book we have that same set of sensibilities in modern guise. One Puritan once said that affliction was a dirty lane to a royal palace, and that is the testimony of this book."

–Douglas Wilson, author of *Evangellyfish* and *Father Hunger*

"This haunting, deeply pondered and beautifully written witness to God enriching a life that has been invaded byh bewildering and seemingly destructive distress carries great power, and will bring peace and hope to persons in trouble."

–J.I. Packer, author of *Knowing God*

SOJOURNER
SONGS

To My Parents

who are "fire-flies in the hollow of the hills."
−Helene Morange

Contents

SONGS AT NIGHTFALL

SONGS FOR THE NIGHT WATCH

SONGS FOR SUNRISE

SCRIPTURE PASSAGES FOR SOJOURNERS

A Note To The Reader

   If humanity can be divided into two groups–those
who love poetry and those who don't–I am clearly on the
side of those who do. But it wasn't always so. I met a real
poet once, when I was younger. He worked a forgettable 9-5
job, but he told me that his real job was being a poet. I still
remember the small gag reflex in the back of my throat. I
pitied him as a kind of second-rate citizen, ill-equipped to
pull his economic weight; a drifter without any real ambition
who probably dropped out of high school and desperately
needed a title to justify his existence. So much wasted poten-
tial.

   The truth is, poetry was more like a strange un-
cle than a friend for most of my life. I dodged poetry and

sympathized with those who found poetry ornery, peculiar, unwilling to confess its meaning in a clear, simple formula, even under the most grueling interrogation. Reading poetry with any strict structure was a grind, and any poetry liberated from such forms struck me as a waste of time.

For me and those like me, mystery is fine so long as it doesn't come clothed in poetry. I did not know that a complex world demands poets willing to dislocate common language and startle the soul, willing to tell the truth from a slant, willing to breach the inner life. I did not know that poetry must be "a raid on the inarticulate" (T.S. Eliot, "East Coker") and I did not know that a poet's purpose is to "transmute his personal and private agonies into something rich and strange" (ibid, *Personal Essays*).

Not until I suffered a massive health collapse did I finally discover the friendship of poetry. It was there all along, untouched by time, ready to serve, stir the soul, shift the gaze, or strike a match in the heart. Poetry is written by commoners who know what it's like to suffer. And they're not afraid to talk honestly about it. They know what it's like to enjoy simple, common pleasures, too, and they enjoy waking us, complete strangers, to those gifts of moment.

19

I have discovered rather late in life that poetry is a necessity, like our need to be touched. Garrison Keillor taught me that simple fact in his introduction to *Good Poems for Hard Times*. That short essay is, in my humble opinion, a nearly perfect invitation to the world of poetry and most of my thoughts in this note to you are borrowed with humble gratefulness to him. He reminded me that poetry is not a riddle to be solved, but a rendering of gravity, grace, and beauty that lends courage to strangers. Poetry does that for me. *Garrison Keillor*

How thankful I am for poetry's generosity in that regard and for its patience with me. It's true, poetry is sometimes ornery, peculiar, and difficult to understand, but so are most of my closest friends. And, like those friends, poetry that matters is never smug. It's never evasive or slippery, coded or disingenuous. Poetry is more direct than most of our daily conversations, more sincere than the rabble noise of politicians or sitcoms, more comforting than the common cliches on our billboards and virtual spaces. Have you noticed how rare it is to hear someone offer you something from the heart? Poetry that matters always does.

Good poems, like good people, are earnest. Like those people, they touch our lives in their own, unique way. Gerard Manley Hopkins, in "As Kingfishers Catch Fire," wrote that "each mortal thing does one thing and the same/...goes itself; myself it speaks and spells/ crying What I do is me: for that I came." Like other mortal things, a poem exists as a unique thing. It leaves the poet and walks through the world as itself, crying "What I do is me!"

So it was in my deepest need that I found courage and hope and perspective in the bold, heart-felt writing of Gerard Manley Hopkins, Li-Young Lee, T.S. Eliot, Theodore Roethke, Rainer Maria Rilke, William Wordsworth, Billy Collins, and Mary Oliver. Each, in his or her own way, loosed the chains of my self-absorption.

But more than all these, I found comfort and aid in the Christian scriptures. C.S. Lewis suggested that we read stories to know we're not alone. I read the Bible to know that I'm not alone. During my health collapse, certain scripture passages spoke radiantly and sympathetically into my desert place, so I collected *some* of those passages and included them in this volume of poetry.

The poems in this book are largely inspired by these

passages. I did not attempt to write poetic translations or poetic renderings of those verses. I simply wrote to capture what I felt was the central spirit of the passage and its poignancy in my life. I tried to write in imitation of the psalmist, who bared his heart—all its doubts, shame, fears, ecstasies, and shams—before God. David was a poet king who recognized his weakness and his status as a sojourner. For that reason, the Psalms are a comfort for those of us who feel alone in our frail and wandering humanity.

That comfort is not limited to the Psalms; the entire Bible is for sojourners. Yes, it provides directions and rules for the road, but more than that, it describes a context for their stories—where they came from and where they are going—and songs to sing along the way. It also provides promises for sojourners who feel lost in a desert: "Blessed are those whose strength is in you, whose hearts are set on pilgrimage. As they pass through the Valley of Weeping, they make it a place of springs; the autumn rains also cover it with pools. They go from strength to strength, till each appears before God in Zion" (Psalm 84:5-7).

These poems are an attempt to turn my valley of weeping into a place of springs. Many of them recapture my deepest feelings of despair during that health collapse so many years ago. I wrote them for me and for those whose hearts, like mine, are set on pilgrimage. May this book be a pool of fresh water in your desert place. May it help you go from strength to strength beneath the open sky of God's grace.

Finally, some readers might wonder why I chose to write these poems in free verse. Honestly, after I finally came around to poetry, I still harbored a prejudice against free verse. Convinced that the sonnet was the high point of poetic expression, I disdained free verse as the irreverent, slipshod child of a post-modern age. I preferred the simple, easily identifiable external restrictions of the sonnet and overlooked the more subtle, more complex, internal discipline of free verse. In my prejudice, I failed to recognize the limitations and guiding principles of free verse as an art form.

Poetry is the precise, rhythmic, playfulness of words. The seeming unrestraint of free verse belies a precise, poetic rigor which demands a metaphysical awareness from both poet and reader. As such, meaning in free verse, as in life, is found in more than words. Even the space around words

23

carries meaning. Isn't the silence between spoken words as significant to conversation and relationship as the words themselves? Or consider the visual arts: negative space in a painting is equally important to positive space in the cohesion and meaning of a piece. I find in free verse a preferable rhythm and line intention which allows the mind and heart to breathe, undistracted by so many of the formalities found in other kinds of poetry.

I have organized these poems in four sections which follow the liturgical hours. For many Christians through the centuries, the liturgical hours marked and anchored the hours of each day with prayer. It seemed natural to structure this poetry collection upon the practices of those who recognized their status as sojourners. Because we are sojourners, our experiences run the gamut of deep despair to buoyant exultation. The first section of poetry recalls the works of God and assesses the present, the second section largely anticipates the long night ahead, the third section wrestles with the despair of suffering, and the final poems reflect the hope offered by the rising sun. However you read these poems, by reading straight through or by selecting those poems which fit your circumstances, I hope they serve as good company on your journey.

I offer these poems as a peace offering to those whom I have loved and to those whom I have hurt. Perhaps a spiritual alchemy will transmute my personal agonies and private joys into something rich and strange for you, dear reader. As they are, I gift them to you.

These are the poems of a pilgrim. These are sojourner songs.

Ben Palpant, 2016

lamp–lighting songs at evening

———————◆———————

Bright Fire

I sat on stone
and waited.
I wept into wind
alone.

Indefinite gloom loomed
until I saw him, my liberator,
running, singing.
His song lifted my soul high,
soaring with wide wing,
stirred by Hope.

Sing to me, O my troubadour.
Let your songs echo
in the halls of my loneliness,
even my shame,
so that I may sing back
and, perhaps, learn by heart.
Perhaps.

Graced is the man who locks eyes with you,
who does not dodge the reckoning.
He shall walk on water,

though it swells.
He will not loiter with the proud,
nor relish the shim-sham dance
of the damned.

Your works, O Lord, astonish me!
You, composer, conductor, star.
You, a kaleidoscope of love.
You are my horizon and my here.
You are the moon to the tides of my heart.

You gather glory,
a bright fire,
and light up this dreary day-to-day.
You invade my valley of dry bones
singing a song of healing,
great God!

This is the glad refrain of my dreams;
this, the theme of my sojourner songs.

Inspired by Psalm 40:1-5 (page 152)

Death And His Friends

This is my story.
This is me:
I searched the ground,
scanned the sky.
I shook the bottle of self-reliance,
long drained, over my dry lips.
I mumbled prayers like a drunkard
and fell down the stairs of disenchantment.

He leaned his ear toward my cry.
He heard my shuffling and my sobs.
He saw my crumpled body, legs akimbo
and came.

The voices now are gone;
death and his friends ran naked.
We watched them flee across the plains.
Unravel their lies, O Lord!
Wipe their names from every stone,
leaf, and heart.
My heart.
Sweet Jesus! You gaze upon me.
Tenderly.

Gladly.

Firmly.

Now.

This poor man staggered under shame,

but you heard my cry and came.

Now you walk so closely,

I hear you breathing.

I bless your name endlessly!

Your praise eternally echoes

in the cavern of my mouth.

Come.

What other boast do I have

than in my strong deliverer?

And who else will take up his praise

than the contrite and humbled heart?

Inspired by Psalm 34 (page 153)

Blessed Are the Broken Brave

When he saw the throng,
he climbed the mountain.
We followed just in case
he scattered gold dust on the wind.
He fingered dirt
with carpenter's hands
and spoke:

Rich are desert dwellers,
bedouin hearts
with empty hands asking "Why?"
They shall dig cisterns in the sand
and rain will fall from blackened sky.

Blessed are the broken brave,
leaning into grief.
Tears will slake their thirst
and solace find them
at the end of their worst.

Glad are the fortunate few,
content with two loaves
and three perch.

They shall lift eyes to heaven
and own the earth.

Rich are sparrow spirits,
craning their necks
to swallow Light.
They shall be filled,
even at night.

Blessed are those who care.
Look, even now
the forlorn and forgotten
gather one thousand strong
to serve like grace-laden footmen.

Rich is the man who sees God
in the wilderness.
He is a spring.
Pitch your tent and plant your heart
where the olive and fig trees are flourishing.

Happy is the peacemaker.
He carries olive branch in hand
and a coal on his tongue.
Gladness covers him, robe-like,

though his feet have trod in dung.

Blessed are the crucified innocent
who spread their arms
to hold the world.
They will sail heaven's seas
with their hearts unfurled.

Inspired by Matthew 5:3-10 (page 155)

Julie

I remember the squat, white house
and the steps,
and the peeling paint on the porch,
and the piled dishes in the kitchen sink,
and the half-cut tomato on the counter,
where Julie lived.
The house with a permanently open door.
The house patched together over a hundred years.
The house with nothing to boast of
except for Julie
who shared her small plate of chicken,
who offered a little beauty,
who gave some time,
while songs leapt
                    out of
                            her
                                pockets
to sing in the eaves
of my heart
                    like goldfinches.

An obscure house
on a forgotten street

in a small town,
but there were few places I'd rather be
than in the house
where Julie lived
and laughed
                    for me.

I Have Held Time's Shell

I have held time's shell
to my ear and heard
the deep, endless, reverberations
of God's voice,
wave upon wave.

But now I stand
at this intersection,
bombarded
by horns and heralds,
herded
by small demands,
propelled
by petty problems,
distracted
by advertisements shouting toothpaste promises,

trying to remember
what it felt like
to hear the tide
of God's voice rolling
wave upon wave.

The Coming of God

On this side of the Red Sea,
when the ground quaked
beneath Egypt's flying chariots,
we heard the victory cry of her warriors
and felt the hot shame
of panic
creep into our loins
and unman us
as we fled
on broken sandals
over mollusks and barnacles.

That was a day of God's coming.

When God arrived,
just like at Horeb,
we stood,
mouths gaping,
hands limp at our sides
like a colony of penguins,
and witnessed the coming of God.
On the other side of abject fear
we watched the laughing waves

swallow our dread.

Something inside us trembled.

Something inside us whispered,
"Behold, our God!"

My Heart, Like a Pheasant

Dear Friend,

My heart,
like a pheasant flushed,
thundered from the thicket
        when you accused me.

Furious in flight,
my startling display of red rage
in the gray regularity of the day
        must have surprised you.

If you suddenly sat down
on your haunches
to wait,
or started barking in alarm,
or plunged after me
through the tall grass,
                I'll never know.

                I was long gone.

Friendship

So many things came easier
when I was a boy.
Sleep, for example.
Or climbing trees.
Or friendship.

These days,
I stare at the towering trunk
and tangled web of limbs,
and wonder how to start.
Who will clasp fingers,
palms up,
to give me a boost?

Is it you,
the surprise of God?

One limb at a time.
There. Like that.

Now here, take my hand.

Fly-Fishing on the St. Joe

All this,
cut by waters
since time immemorial–
clear, turquoise, deep–
cliffs steep,
stooped;
moss and leaning
green.

You and me,
lines curled out,
behind, and
out again;
rhythmic and
soft
   landing
      of
        fly;
rocks piled like
loaves of bread;
this water,
like wine.

If time could stop,

freeze frame
our communion,
I think I could let go

of my dreams,
of the endless lists,
of unfulfilled hopes,
of projects,
of agenda items,

even the unresolved
conflicts
of my soul.

I could leave my questions
on the table

glad.

The Rope of Love
(To My Eldest Daughter, Upon Her Eighth Birthday)

My fair and dandled daughter, one with sun
And moon and sky, to you I write with hope
Today reminds us all of why you run:
Of laughter, brook, the pony's neigh, and rope
Of love. With all your little might, you lift
The heavy, sodden, sullen, shape of me
With smile and stroke of chin, and upward tilt
Of face. You bear the stuff of story. Be
Newmade of God. Each day find strength and grace
To know his mercies soft, to know his hand
So strong. To God belongs your all, so face
His face with Joy. He calls you daughter. Stand.
 No more let frown nor sorrow weigh you down,
 But climb up here and hug my neck around.

Song of the Desert

I didn't say it,
you did.
And now I'm leaning against a stone,
huddled in a sliver of shade,
staring at a sand-scape,
sun-stroked already,
and wondering what you meant
when you said,
"Alleluia is the song of the desert."

A conversation with Thomas Merton

You Have Thrown the Bolts to My Heart

O Lord!
You have surveyed my lands.
You have scaled the rock-face
of my ambitions.
You have plumbed my depths
and inspected all my caves.
I have no dark corner,
neither attic nor cellar,
unexplored by you.
You have even thrown the bolts to my heart
and opened the secret door
to my covert chamber
and weighed the confidential things
that I buried in a steel box
in a concealed safe
there.

O Lord,
you know my routines,
my waking and sleeping.
You know the worn path
of my thoughts
and my tongue.

Even my hamster wheel of worry
is well-known to you.
When I stop running
to listen,
I feel your hands behind
and in front
and see the imprint of your protection
in the sands around me.

O Lord,
where could I hide
if I wanted to?
And I'm not saying that I do,
but still.

If I cover my face,
you are there.
If I sleep with thieves and brigands,
you are there.
If I climb two-hundred and nine floors
to the top of Burj Khalifa
and share lobster caviar
or goldleaf-wrapped sushi
with the affluent or vain,
you are there.

Even if I descend into the ghetto

of my personal hell

to choke

again

on regret,

you are there.

O Lord, how can this be?

How is it that my happiness

and my fear

are both alike to you?

How can it be, O Lord,

that my dread is nothing but

the prelude

to a new song you sing

in the morning light

of a new day? O Lord!

Inspired by Psalm 139:1-12 (page 156)

It Is I, God

All these thirsty settlers
have hired water diviners
from east to west,
but the land is dry.
Their tongues fail.
They can't even cry out.

I hear their pregnant silence.
I hear their suffering.
I hear the groans of their hearts.

No longer
will they sit beneath the Joshua tree
and scratch in the dirt
with broken sticks.
Neither they nor their children.
I will plant the Cypress tree
and the Pine.
The Bullrush and Bird-of-paradise
shall bloom
bright.

I will break open the earth
with my splitting maul

and they will look down,

to see water

seeping up

in the desert.

This will I do

as gift,

as grace,

as proof

of power

that it is I, God,

who did this thing.

It is I who broke the earth open

like an orange

and flooded their lives

with the juice of generosity.

It is I, God!

Inspired by Isaiah 41:17-20 (page 158)

songs at nightfall

———●◆●———

Remember the Time

Remember the time
when he spoke
and something quickened
in your bones
like a match struck in the dark?
You picked up that stretcher
and strode into a new day,
under a laughing sun,
before a hundred craning necks.

Remember the time
when he broke the bread
and then vanished
and you gasped
because you knew him?
That wry smile
like a wink
and a welcome.

Remember the time
you felt the ground
against your face?
Damnation crackled the air

like electrical wires.
You crawled to his feet,
waiting.
And then he said, "Rise."
And you looked
afraid
but they were gone
and you were alone
together.
Forgiven.
Safe.
Free.

Remember the time
you wailed
long into the night?
"She is dead!
My girl
is dead."
And he said,
like the voice of reason,
"She is only asleep."
On the sudden,
she was serving you
biscuits and tea

with two cubes of sugar
just the way you like it.

Remember the time
you said, "No,"
instead of "Yes"?
The rooster crowed
as promised
and you felt regret,
the great worm in your belly,
until he came to you
while you dissolved in shame,
calling you
friend,
rock,
which you could not imagine.
But you were together.
Forgiven.
Brave.
Free.

Remember the time
he untied his sandals,
disrobed,
and we saw
his shoulder blades,

the back of his knee?
He took basin and towel,
and washed our feet:
calluses,
broken nails,
and sweat.
And we knew,
because it was just his way,
that we could walk a thousand miles
in a desert,
a life-time if need be,
so long as he washed our feet
like this
at the end.

Remember.
The time is still here
and not yet. Not yet.

Inspired by Psalm 103 (page 183)

Come, Sit, Eat

Come.
Here is my home,
humble,
happy,
most of the time.
Don't mind the mess.

Sit.
Here is my wooden table,
scratched,
heavy with food,
leaning with memories.

Eat.
Here is forgiveness.
Here is healing.
Here is dignity.

Here, have some of my gladness.

A Continent of Trees

Standing on my narrow shoreline,
staring at a continent of trees,
I am reminded of my small self
and humble backpack of supplies.
What will be the use
of my pocket knife and
borrowed flashlight
in such wildwood?
How will a half-eaten sandwich
vitalize my soul
for the immense wilderness?

Countless fears claw inside:
fang and talon;
the maniacal eye
and cackle in the dark;
the serpent's venom
and looping, sliding body,
squeezing, squeezing.
The myriad black days
alone,
    wondering,
    wandering,

my mind

comes

unglued.

I will wait for my strider,

my path finder,

who will clear the way,

leave markers,

light a flare,

instruct,

conduct,

attend,

guard me

through the perilous land.

He will come.

He has promised.

Inspired by Psalm 130 (page 189)

Tell Me, Friend

If ditch-digging has worked you over,
left you clutching your knees,
dog-tired, spitting in a cup,
then tell me, friend,

how will you brave the warhorse
weighted with plate armor,
trained to trample,
bones built for battle?

If you languish
in your leisure hours,
floating on calm waters,
inventing countless causes to complain,
then tell me, friend,

how will you survive the white squall
sudden, savage, silent,
decisive?
How?

Inspired by Jeremiah 12:5 (page 159)

Songs of Scattered Stars

Listen, Jacob had his worries.
They flapped,
croaked like
jackdaws in his
brain. Restless
in a weary
land of rocks and tamarisk
trees and night arrived,
bushwhacking
his thoughts and
highjacking his schedule.

So he found a stone,
low and flat like a pillow,
and stretched out his one wool blanket
and lay down
with his head on rock
and tried to sleep,
turning this way and that
on his bed of earth.

Dreams came slowly:
a wooden ladder leaning on the sky,
an angel or two

and then a host
climbing down
and up
more than he could count.
Strange.
And why?

Then a face leaned over the ladder
and spoke poetry of promise,
songs of scattered stars.

Something sparked in his brain.

The flock of birds fled, shrieking,
and Jacob awoke with ground made green in his mind,
the whole world suddenly fertile with divine.

How shall I say it?
It was as if he stood in the desert,
neck deep in a spreading supernal sea of surprise,
and he cried out, "Surely this is God's house
and I did not know it!
Surely this is the gateway of heaven!"

Listen, so much for Jacob.
Here I am flopped down in my own desert,

exhausted,

restless,

bemoaning my outcast state.

Here I am with my fair share of jackdaws

pecking relentlessly.

What have I to do with Jacob?

What has Jacob to do with me

and these three pots of geraniums?

Is it true, this poetry of promise?

Is this grizzled carpet a quarter note

in God's song of scattered stars?

Is this battered chair

pregnant with the divine?

Could it be?

And what if I am chasing the wind

at the gateway of heaven?

Beach Combing

It's certainly not every day,
but sometimes.

Sometimes
I feel like a beach comber
who wakes to walk the shoreline of memory
and keeps bending over to pick up the ocean's trash
and throw it back.
Odds and ends:
a spool of fishing line,
a door knob, an old tire.

Mostly I find dead fish lining the beach
with discolored skin
hanging in threads,
infested.
I keep throwing them all back and
rinsing my hands in the salt water,
but

in the morning,
their heavy bodies
depress the damp sand again

as though I slept through a tidal wave of stink.
Their eyes stare aimlessly,
covered by spreading sallow mucus
like the white of an egg cooking in the pan.

I'd like to welcome guests
to walk the beach of my memory,
but I'm afraid they'll slip on all the dead fish
and scuttle away like crabs to find a hole and hide.
I'm afraid they'll discover
that my ocean-front property,
contrary to all the brochures,
is actually an open grave
sometimes.

Who will rise in the pre-dawn darkness
to stride my shoreline,
gather these carcasses,
toss them into the back of his truck,
and drive toward the horizon
to burn them on a distant,
ceremonial pyre?
When will I wake
to find a beach populated by
sandpipers

and my waters splashing
with bluefish?
When will I watch the crashing waves,
undistracted by the odor of death?

Maybe this morning
I will bring my beach chair,
just in case today is the day
I get to sit
and breathe.

Inspired by Psalm 71 (page 191)
and Isaiah 63 (page 195)

So Here I Stand

O Lord,
come running.
In the day of desperation
your name is on my lips.
I cling to it when swords come clashing
and whisper it when the jackals
snicker and prowl here,
amongst the dead.

So here I stand.

What or whom should I fear?
You have proven that you save
your chosen ones.
Indeed, you answer
out of holy heaven
with right arm flexed,
fists furious,
feet flying.

Some say, "The Lord helps those who help themselves."
Others say, "I can help myself."
I say, "God help me or I die!"

The name of the Lord
is my lone salvation.

I am purposed,
my heart shot like an arrow.
Fulfill my aim
and I will shout and leap at your coming.
For your great name is my anthem.
Only you can answer my cry.

The schemer.
The miser.
The brash.
The *ubermensch*.
Behold,
they lick the dust!

Save me, O my King!

Remember your promises.
Remember my cause and my sacrifices.
Send your infantry
armed
and your horsemen

thundering.
Take us by surprise.

I stand,
vertical in the wasteland
and wait.

Come running,
O Lord!

I Taste My Tears

The calf bakes under the sun,
frets under his yoke.
He twitches nagging flies from his back
again and again.
His mouth is parched
like the earth.
He longs for water.

Why this endless plowing of dry clay?
Why these stones?
Where is the end to weariness?

I, too, long for water,
for living water.
When will I stop plodding,
endlessly plowing
fallow ground?
When will I stand before God,
liberated from this heavy yoke
and the biting horseflies of futility?
I taste my tears day after day
and strain beneath the lash.

O my God!
My soul is mired in the muck of myself.

So I will look to you
in Chelan or
driving up the winding road to St. Maries.
Wandering the Bitteroot Mountains
or the Black Hills,
I will consider God.

Even when night is hot and sullen,
I will think on God
who bathes me in his lovingkindness.
I will remember the songs of salvation
and lift them on the wind.

They are prayers
to the God of my life.

Inspired by Psalm 42 (page 160)

Sacrament of Love

We gather together
in beards and braids,
with broken shoes,
wondering
where the good times went.
A coughing collage
of khaki and blue,
we slouch
to ameliorate the discomfort
of being alive
with arthritis
and tooth infections
and crying babies.

Where did they go,
those days of wine and roses?
We had stretched to hold
more than our share of leisure.
We had filled our mouths
with cassaba melon
and roast beef.
We had passed around
the salted cashews,

toasting health
and long life.

But now,
here we are
holding a pinch of bread,
waiting
in our brokenness
and hunger
at the Lamb's table.
A sad turn of affairs?
Perhaps.
But it cost us nothing,
there's plenty to go around,
and those who eat
are filled.

They say
you get what you pay for.
Sometimes. But
what about bread of life?
What about a cup
of living water?
Could it be?
We paid nothing.
This is the sacrament of love!

Sometimes the good times
are small,
and now,
and simple,
and forever.

Inspired by Numbers 11:4-6 (page 186)

The Stranger

"Be prepared for The Stranger
who knows how to ask questions," he said.
"Be prepared for The Stranger coming from Edom,
traveling in the greatness of his strength."

And I remembered stories
of a man loping down the road
on bare feet,
girded by a towel,
wearing a crown–
a man who could unravel my soul
like a thread
and swing me into the ocean of stars.
They say that conversation always brewed
like a storm around his head.
They say he came to climb a tree
and die with splinters in his hands.

"I perceive approaching
The Rock. The Watcher. The Stranger," he said.

Then he smiled in that charged way of his
and I was afraid,
and confused, and

a little indecisive,

like a mouse in an open field

when a shadow passes overhead.

I started

scurrying this way

and that

while the sound of my little heart

beating,

beating,

filled the sky.

And then he stood there–

The Stranger.

Rollicking.

O, my God!

He reached down,

plucked me by the tail,

and flung me into the ocean of stars.

Inspired by T.S. Eliot's, "Choruses From The Rock"

and by Isaiah 40 (page 217)

God Save Me

 God save me from this,

my daily grind:

the intemperate racing

of my mind.

Deliver me from lusts

that ruin and lay waste:

flesh,

serenity,

praise,

and haste.

Hard To Believe

I have a hard time remembering,
an even harder time believing

that you are sculptor supreme
who forms me
along a mysterious armature—
divine dignity—
who shapes my becoming,
who wields his hammer
and aims his chisel
to unearth beauty.

You fashioned my knees
and the creases of my palms.
You sanded down these stooped shoulders
and know these weak hams.
You have traced the inside of my ribs
with your finger.

You sat in the darkness of my mother's womb
and spoke my days
one heartbeat at a time.
And since the day of my birth,

you have escorted me
into each day hand-crafted
affectionately, tenderly,
gladly.

Who would look on this sculpture,
lean back, cock his hat,
and say, "It is good"?
You, my Lord!

You grind my sin into a powder
with the rock of your Son.
You dress me in white samite.

Sometimes I have a hard time remembering,
an even harder time believing.

Inspired by Psalm 139:13-24 (page 162)

I'm Willing Lord

I'd sacrifice the farm:
Every goat and unruly rooster.
The cattle.
Yes, the mules.
All slaughtered on a wooden plank
blood-soaked.
If you wanted.

I'd pile the meat
in the field and torch it.
Black smoke billowing
for hours.
Burnt flesh reeking the sky.
If you wanted.

But you said, "Stop."
You said, "Keep the farm.
Give me, instead,
a humble heart,
a broken spirit,
a willing will."
So here I am
slopping out the pens.

Later, I'll pitch hay.
Tomorrow, I'll keep framing the house,
the best I can, and
before nightfall,
I'll cross the field
carrying hammer and nails
to help my neighbor
roof his shed.
Maybe we'll share a meal
before I take the long walk
home
through the dark
to sleep
and start again
at sunrise.

I'm willing, Lord. You want it.
It is not too much to ask as thanks
for hope and a future.

Inspired by Psalm 51:15-19 (page 167)

Fear Not

"Fear not," he said.
"Be glad, for the Lord favors you."

But "fear not" is a hard task.
Give me a hundred lashes.
Give me a bed of coals.
Give me martyrdom.
But "fear not,"
I cannot.

And how can I believe
the Lord favors me
on those days when
shame holds my towel,
and offers the car keys,
even opens the door?

I remembered
the years swallowed whole
by Lust and her sisters,
Avarice and Ambition.
I remembered
the hand of God

pressed down on my back
until I suffocated in my sheets,
so when God pours out promises,
it is a strange epiphany.

The rain falls.
The fig tree
and the vine flourish.
The wheat does not run out,
nor does the wine,
nor the oil.

All these blessings are proof,
God's proof
to me
that he stands here,
present,
taking my shame,
holding my heart,
even opening the day,
lavishing goodness.

Just because.

What am I to do,

standing neck deep
in blessing?

Fear not. Be glad.

Lord, I believe.
Help, Thou, my unbelief!

Inspired by Joel 2:21-27 (page 187)

This Is Me, Finally

I have set my weapons down,
the long range guns
and my favorite dagger
useful in hand-to-hand combat.
I have stripped off my armor,
even the chainmail,
and now I'm left with my many masks,
all of which I place before you now,
I think.

I have checked all my pockets
to see if there are any shams hiding,
and come up empty,
so this is it.
This is me.
Finally.
Vulnerable.

No more pretending
or posturing.
No more swagger
or insincere jocularity.
I won't even pretend to be smart,

which we both know is an ongoing sham
you have patiently tolerated
long enough.

This is me now,
holding in hand
a fragile seed,
my heart.
It's yours
with the rest of me
and the baggage piled at your feet.

Before I Lay Me Down To Sleep

Before I lay me down to sleep,
My heart I give for you to keep.

For all my sins, both old and new,
Forgive them, Lord, and make me true.

Lord, you are mindful of my fears
That, in the dark, I overhear.

Stand guard, O King, and stay awake
To hear my cry for your name's sake.

Remind me often through the night,
That nothing e'er escapes your sight.

So what I do and what I say,
Cleanse me, guide me on the way.

Please, Lord, speak even in my dreams.
And fill my mind with cleansing streams.

Then, when I wake tomorrow morn,
Give me new hope and vision born.

songs for the night watch

Is This You, Lord?

O Lord,
you have set me in a dark place
where I turn the crank
on grief:
a jack-in-the-box
that jumps me,
    again
        and again.

No, it's worse than that.

Grief, to me,
is an armed bandit
in an alley
of bewilderment.

Grief blocks escape
and breaks bones
with a metal pipe.

Grief robs me
of everything
but desolation

and leaves me
to gag, groan.

Is this you,
O Lord?
Or something else?

I am ambushed
again
and torn to pieces.
Something mashes my face
with its boot's heel.
These teeth, broken
with rocks.
I sit here
spitting blood in the dirt.

Something small inside
still
voices
and I hear it
barely
whisper:

"You are good,

O Lord,
and faithful.
You are all I need.
I wait in my despair.
I wait for you
here."

Remember.
Remember my suffering,
O Lord.
Remind me
of your mercies
and compassion,
which never fail,
which are new
every morning.

Every
morning.

Inspired by Lamentations 3:1-24 (page 205)

Despair Has Come

The capital city of my heart
is dead, is dead.
Sight of strong lords and light,
lies buried.
Ash and rubble.
In the choking silence
I wander with a spade, digging
here and digging there
to uncover limb, key,
broken plate.

Lonely.
Muttering.
A perplexed king
searching for his dreams.

Despair arrived
silently,
suddenly,
smothering the children,
even the brave warriors: my hopes.
I heard no cries in the night.
No firebrands. No pistol shots.

At evening, I lay down confidently,

the lights of my city warm,

with many reasons to wake

and work, but

morning dawned rust red,

drifting smoke,

smell of charred wood.

Who will marshal the old forces

that lie ten thousand dead?

Who will raise the beleaguered banner,

once bright,

and brandish it high to snap in the wind?

Do you remember when we walked

together

under the gibbous moon

and you said, "I will stand fast with God

as a man will stand,

rooted like a tree beneath the stars,"

and I said, "I will remain with you"?

And we swore

constancy,

endurance,

despite the strength of tides

or force of wind;

to fight—

even with our teeth and fists—

if the shield wall scattered

and our blades broke.

Do you remember?

But you have slipped from my hands

with my resolve

and I am abandoned to this throne of futility,

a king of shreds and patches.

I'm trying.

I'm trying.

But how to raise the dead?

Inspired by Habakkuk 3:17-19 (page 209)

97

i don't approve

your plans O Lord
for me
feel mangled
tonight
i don't approve
tonight
i can't breathe
tonight
i'm huddled in the corner
harboring disintegration
tonight
my sight is narrowed
to a three inch space
in my brain
where i try to remember
names
phone numbers
and that one time
when i stood in a field
of fireflies
rising
out of tall grass
mystic

grace

your plans for me are prosperous

but tonight
i wallow
and i can't
bring myself to confront
the broad-shouldered beast
they call
tomorrow
baring its teeth

for me
and my white-knuckled heart
O Lord
prosper
us

tonight

At the Still Point

I carry a satchel
stuffed with notes from a prophet.
I read each,
one at a time,
on lonesome nights,
under darkening skies.

"Fear multiplies exponentially
with each glance
over the shoulder."

"He who runs
shall get trampled
by fear's phantoms."

"He who fears
shall be like one standing naked
and alone in an open field."

"He who seeks salvation
must turn and run toward fear."

"He who clings

to the still point
of the turning wheel
shall be saved."

So now I sit
with my satchel
and rest until morning.
I wait
and watch
for the dawn
here,
at the still point
of this whirling wheel.

Inspired by Isaiah 30:15-25 (page 203)

We Are the Lost Boys

We are the lost boys.
We are the terrified,
leaning together
in the dusk and doom. Alas!
Our waggery
and jocund backslapping
of a few hours ago
is meaningless
as rowing against a gale.

Movement without purpose,
sound without meaning;

This is the wooded land.
This is the fog shrouded land.
Here, branches yield no light
and no clear path through the underbrush.
Here we grope together sightless,
banging a broken flashlight on our legs,
to no avail.

We wait for approaching night
huddled back-to-back,
facing the inscrutability of silence

and darkness
punctuated by scurrying animal feet
in the dry leaves.

We are the lost boys
rubbing sticks furiously to kindle a fire,
hoping to encircle ourselves with sparks
because we heard a branch snap
somewhere in the dark
and glimpsed the fleeting eyes
of a creature we dare not name.

Between the now
and the not yet,
between the yes
and the maybe,
falls the Shadow.

I have come to set the world on fire.

Between the anticipation
and the terror,
between the stillness
and the spasm,
falls the Shadow.

And how I wish it were already burning!

We are the scared boys
tormented by phantoms,
afraid to sit,
unable to run.
We are alone
together.

I am the light of the world.

Is this the way the world ends?
Canine teeth clamped down on the neck
and a silent terror?
Not even a bang, just a whimper?
Who will deliver us from the Shadow?
Who will deliver us from us?

He who follows me
Shall not walk in darkness
But have the light of life.

Inspired by Isaiah 50:10-11 (page 168)

and T.S. Eliot's "The Hollow Men"

My Onion Heart

Peel back the layers
of my onion heart
and we will both weep.

I'd Rather Be Alone

I'd rather be alone
reading poetry by the light of a broken lamp,
or growing cabbages
and scraping mud off my boots in the rain.
Maybe I could map the garden spider's web
and call myself a silk cartographer.
Or I could press my fingers into the dark loam
and let it cake beneath my nails.

I would be happy then, I think.

But a dried mud they call life
obscures my vision and blocks my pores
and I am bound by a web spun by those who
consume bewildered men.
I have no time to trace the web,
or sit beneath a downpour with a lamp
in the middle of my cabbage patch.
Alone.

Freefall For Fun

Up here,
north of the maddening crowd,
snow falls fresh
unstained
powder.
I watch
flakes
drift
free
for fun.

That is how I want to be,
O Lord.
Fresh,
unstained.
Freefall for fun. But

I recall rounding the bend last week,
my car's headlights flooding the closing
moments of a death match:
a mangled mule deer
broken-backed,
convulsing

wild-eyed.

Split jaw.

Spilled intestines.

Fetid air

thick with odor of blood.

And the sound,

a gargled desperation

I am, O Lord.

Mangled, wild-eyed.

Sin spilling stench.

Do not drag me off the road,

into tall grass,

to put a bullet in my brain.

Please. O Lord, whisper

promises. Wrap your blanket

of love around me.

Set these bones,

every vertebrae.

Stitch me whole.

Wash me. I will be clean.

Purge me. I will be pure.

Set me on my feet

to frolic like a fawn
free,
fresh,
for fun.

O Lord,
you can.

Inspired by Psalm 51:1-13 (page 213)

Nothing In My Pockets

It's true.
I'm the man
who wears affliction
like a garment—
God-gifted.

Bitterness and grief
hang on me
day and night.
I have nothing
in my pockets—
     except these prayers.

Inspired by Psalm 102 (page 164)

Death or Deliverance

I was seven years old,
maybe eight,
when I first nearly drowned.
I remember strong arms lifting.
Wet and worn. Me.

I have nearly drowned since,
but nothing like today.

I woke this morning
with my mind mired in the soft clay
of a stretching marshland.
No branches to grab.
No strong arms in sight.
My hands, limp and cold.

I have craned my neck.
Only lips and nostrils
reach above the water,
for now, but
I feel the water rising,
or me,
sinking.

Despair is slow slide,
gradual cessation of blood flow
in veins.
I will die here,
forgotten,
just another body,
another pale, frozen face
staring vacantly.

Who will remember my name?
Who will tell my story?
Who will see me here?
Who will lift me,
pull me,
drag me out
with the sucking sound
of liberation?

I cannot even cry for help.
I can only stand still
and wait
for death
  or deliverance.

Inspired by Psalm 69 (page 169)

Gladness Gone

Gladness gone!
It was taken in the prime of life
and I wept.
I sat down on a wooden chair
and spoke to myself, saying,
"I shall not see the Lord today.
And likely not tomorrow.
I shall reach the end of my days
having waited in vain.
I am the endless plaything of a lion.
He gnaws me in his jaws and clubs me
like a rubber ball.
From midnight to midnight,
I am unraveled."

So I balanced on the roof peak of my heart
like a swallow
and called into mighty winds
with my small bird song.
The wind buffeted and my eyes winced,
weary.

What shall I say?

He composed my story
and comforts me in it.
So I live the story
page by page,
carefully.

I will not forget brokenness
nor the taste of wormwood;
indeed, such memory is life to my spirit
for the sojourner will find peace in pain.
There, at the end of my rope,
you waited
and fastened me to the mountain
of yourself.

Now I am secured,
alive and awake.
Now I tell this story to my children
and we sing songs together
and warm our hearts
at the hearth of Hope.

Inspired by Isaiah 38:11-20 (page 173)

Geese

Yesterday,
a good four or five weeks late,
I heard geese call out of hooded
winter night.
With one hand on the garbage can
I was hauling out to the curb,
I paused, just a moment,
to follow the passing travelers
(maybe three of them,
or four)
with my ear
and wish them merry flight.

If lost,
or just late because good intentions
to leave on time fell amok,
as they are wont to do with families,
I wished them Godspeed and planted the can
like a broad-breasted sentry by the mailbox.
Then I stood a moment
and leaned into the dark
to hear the geese,
but they were gone

and the stillness returned.

I trudged down the walk,
and up the stairs.
With one hand upon the door,
I leaned my ear into the darkness
just once more,
just to make sure,
and stepped inside.

Shall I Bare My Arms

What can I offer
for the expiation
of a lifetime's sin?

Shall I bear my arms
and count the scars?
Or offer up my son
on an altar built,
stone by stone,
with my own hands?
Or wear a shirt of camel hair?
Or pull out this heart
with my bare hands?

No.
You said, "It is finished."

And I believe you.

So I've brought my mason jar
full of sea glass and a handful of coins
to pour out on your table
as thanks.

songs for sunrise

When I Was Not Looking

I spent a sleepless night
wandering the streets of my mind,
ducking derelict memories,
dodging the barking dogs of my fears,
waiting for dawn.

The sun's rising reminds me
of where I've been
and where I'm going.
Through all my yesterdays,
into all my tomorrows,
you are my God.
I will spend eternity
working out the calculus
of that grace.

So I begin now, this morning.
In the stillness at break of dawn,
I seek you.

Stride into my tedium.
I will sit at your feet
to watch you weave a spell

or conjure water from a rock.

Because your love is better than breath,
let me hear the vigor of your voice.
Because you rescued me
when I was not looking,
I will praise you.

I will lift up my hands
in this desert place.
I will track your voice
on the wind and follow.

I will remember the sleight-of-hand
called Love
and the gradual awareness of mystery
and hope
called God.

Inspired by Psalm 6 (page 208)

Life and Live

Today, I celebrate language:
words
and the gaps between them;
meaning
and the silence in between.
I celebrate nouns and verbs.

Life is a noun, like *bird*.
Live is a verb
for those who look up
and read the noun in the sky
and follow it
until evening.

The Weight of Wonder

I will stand small
beneath starry sky.

I will stoop to carry
the weight of wonder.

I will press my ear to the dust
and listen for the coming footsteps
of my inevitable Lord.

Line upon line,
day unto day,
these are the drilled precepts
of humility;
these, the neat,
articulate lines
on my heart's blackboard.

Why Fret and Gnaw Your Hands?

He stood alone
in the rabble kingdom.
The racket and the roar swelled around him
so he sat down
on a stone
and spoke:

"Why fret and gnaw your hands?
Why squirm on a bed of nails?
Study the gray wagtail
with sunlight bursting
from his chest.
Watch him swoop
to catch color, content
with mayflies,
water,
and air.
Is he not splendid
in his smallness?

And behold blue flax,
delicate and coy.
Or ebullient honeysuckle

with her heart on her sleeve.

Lie down in fields of amber

and walk amongst the clapping trees.

Who robes them in glory?

Who sways them in their dance?

Are you sweating beneath the lash

of Maybe

and Not Yet?

Come,

sit here

on this rock.

Let us wait,

together, and

find God in the waiting.

Now

is enough.

Let tomorrow be

tomorrow."

Inspired by Matthew 6:25-32 (page 190)

For the Sake of God's Fame

What broad sky!
What big, blue tent!
Is it not proof text?

Morning's majesties
and milky way
testify to God
and explicate
his divine craftsmanship
in a universal tongue.

Look at the sun,
rising like an Olympian
to swing across heaven's cerulean hue
for the sake of God's name,
for the sake of God's fame,
and to gladden every beating heart.

And look at me:
a parable,
a breathing proof text,
rising this morning
to chase the sun,

to gladden hearts,

to serve the world,

to bless the children.

For the sake of God's name,

for the sake of God's fame.

Inspired by Psalm 19:1-11 (page 211)

I Cannot Stop My Singing Heart

I cannot stop my singing heart
today
it leapt out of bed
into a day
new-graced

smell the crushed grass
beneath these feet
pine pollen
feel
wind stroke
like a daughter's fingers
on my face

I can't decide
which is decked more glamorously
the poplar
or the aspen
groves
or the finch
splashing
along the rocky shore
glancing up

to measure my intent

and welcome

me

into the dance

like you my love

dappled

freckled fair

priceless pearl

bright-eyed beloved

today

is God-made

I cannot stop this singing heart

Inspired by Psalm 118:24 (page 175)

This Morning Is

This morning is
a gleaming door
opening onto mystery.
Unread.
Inviting.
Clean
  pages
    unbent.

Like a kiss,
an unmistakable doorway
into promise.

Aging

When the sun sets on my life,
how many gravesite goodbyes will have cratered
my heart like a bombed out city,
or like the moon?
Deserted.

Is aging
simply learning to crouch
beneath extinction's alp
in a broken house,
buzzed by gnats of memory
in rooms grown tiresome,
endlessly tripping over forgotten furniture?

Indeed,
loneliness clarifies. But
what if aging is
simply accumulating
small joys
not particularly noteworthy,
left unmeasured,
unrecorded?

The piling clouds.

The corn stalks scratching out a fiddle tune.

The pungent fragrance of apple blossoms
crushed beneath this reckless,
glad toddler clutching my finger.

What if aging is
simply deciphering
the whispered Voice of love,
as it should be,
caressing my ear,
like an enormous Yes?

a conversation with Philip Larkin

Never More

"Never more!" you said,
and so you turned your back on God.
You invested your soul
in miles of asphalt
and a thousand lost golf balls.
You placed your hope in market values
and twenty minutes of virtual smiles.
For what?
For this?
Never more.

Gather all the sticks and twigs
in your desert place.
Stack them together.
Pile all the timbers you can find too
and torch them.
Wait for the billowing smoke
to climb into the sky.

Or light the flare
and fire it into the night.

Or scrawl in the sand your S.O.S.

And if no help arrives by dawn,
the sky doesn't part
and no hand reaches down
to pluck you from your despair,
well then,

make pilgrimage across the sands
of your heart.
Unpack your words
in the presence of God.
Arrange them on the floor
one letter at a time:
"Please. Help. Me."

Then sit.
Listen.
He will speak slowly like
rolling thunder.
Do not fear the rumbling, his voice.
It promises rain
to cracked clay hearts.

He shall say,
"I read your cry eagerly.
I trace my fingers over the letters

with love.
I know the taste of dry ground.
I rain grace upon you
despite your small words
and the fickle heart behind them.
Lift your weary face into the rain.
Sink your roots in dark loam.

Then you shall grow
sycamore strong,
unmoved by the winds of want.
Never more
shall you envy the mannequin
and his blue suede shoes.
Never more
shall you chase horizons
of blinking billboards.
Never more.
For what?
For this."

Inspired by Hosea 14:1-9 (page 215)

We Run in Abundant Fields

In you, Lord,
we lack no good thing.
We run in abundant fields.
Lush. Green.
We graze in pastures flowing
with calm streams.
You revive tired souls
and guide us carefully
because your name is at stake.
Even when we reel, blind,
in the valley of dismay,
we lean into hope,
even (dare I say) eager,
for our shoulders touch your own.

Beat us back
when we wander.
Hook us home
to sit with you
by fire and food.
Set fork and plate,
even with foes looming now.

We stand convinced:

Divine generosity,

profound expressions of love,

follow us all day and night.

And we will wake to the song

you sing in your own house,

familiar as friends now,

because your home is our home.

Yes.

Forever.

Inspired by Psalm 23 (page 176)

137

Hannah's Song

My heart! My heart!
It sings in me
like a child
unabashed.
Full-voiced.
Glad!

Who would condemn me?
Who would try
to haul me onto guilt's gallows,
to hang me
with fear's rope?
Come, my enemy,
carrying noose in hand,
let me gift you with this smile—
even a blessing—
because my champion comes.

There is none like him.

Weigh your words
and deeds
O you proud!

Are they not paper dolls
compared to God?
Weigh your heart
and mind
all you who bow
in the kingdom
of bling and blab.
Are they not tinsel
compared to God?

I once stumbled in anguish;
now I swing
on freedom's wings,
small,
like a wren,
forgotten,
      but lighthearted
   and darting from
limb to limb
       like laughter.

My heart's praise
is mountain spring,
gurgling up from the rocks:
cataract,

cool,

continuous.

My heart's praise

is cacophony of song

clapping on stones.

Listen, my friends!

Listen to the music!

Inspired by I Samuel 2:1–9 (page 177)

You Weren't There

When we stumbled out of Egypt
carrying four hundred years
of oppression on our backs,
we dared not look up
lest we see the disintegration of hope
before our very eyes.
The myths of our people were the brick
and mortar of our hearts,
but we'd grown accustomed to the sky falling
and the smiler with the knife
in the dark.

Surely you can understand, dear friend,
why we twisted the ends of our hair
and kept looking over our shoulders.
Surely you can appreciate the squeeze
of anxiety around our throats.
I see the same bruises on your neck.
I hear the hesitation in your voice.
We share the same dread of the impending,
inevitability of doom, but

you weren't there when the sea parted,

curled up like enormous rhubarb leaves
on either side of us.

You can imagine joy,
waking inside us
like a doe,
cautious:
one foot, then
the next.
You can imagine
the strange alchemical change
born from a sudden mixture of dread
and hope. You can only imagine,
but that will have to do.

Tomorrow
or maybe a year from now
you will taste the miracle of deliverance
and witness the transformation of dread
to hope, pulsing,
robust.
Perhaps you will feel your heart again
for the first time.

Inspired by Psalm 114 (page 210)

Come

All you dragging refugees
suffering from malnutrition
with peeling lips
and bloated bellies,
come!
Here is a glass of milk
and a table filled with cheese,
and greens.
Here is a field of fruit.
Here is lamb and dove.

Why do you spend your last coins
on stones and snakes?
Why keep chewing gravel
and squeezing out venom
from the punctures in your heart?

I offer you food for life.
I offer my life for food.
Come. Take and eat.

Inspired by Isaiah 55 (page 179)

Bear the Beams of Love

i am learning
slowly
how to bear the beams
        of love
and will
happily
share the load,
shoulder to shoulder,
        with you
until,
at the edge of eternity,
we're strong enough to run
        together
        into fields of gold.

To You, A Stranger

To you, a stranger,

I offer these hands, empty
but for the blessing they hold.

I offer these words,
the overflow of my love,
trying to find new ways to say so.

I offer this heart,
driven to desire
togetherness.

I offer you me
still learning to love.

You Are, I Am

I am grass,
>   green today, gone tomorrow.

I am breath,
>   a short exhale in this opera.

I am sheep,
>   bewildered, blundering.

I am soil,
>   cradling seeds.

I am branch,
>   bearing fruit.

I am grape,
>   crushed, oozing joy.

I am builder,
>   measuring a mansion.

I am lantern,
>   held high on a hill in the dark night.

You are good loam,
>   ground of being.

You are singer,
>   fullthroated.

You are shepherd,

strong.
You are sower,
  deliberate.
You are arborist,
  visionary.
You are winemaker,
  artful.
You are rock,
  firm.
You are flame,
  bright.

You are I Am.

Lodestar

I lost my lodestar in the night.
A legion of clouds
scuttled my Polaris
and unstitched the stars.

Now I cross
unfamiliar ground–
a patchwork
of tamaracks,
bunchgrass,
wintered phlox–

beneath slate heavens
that slide down the sky,
settle in stone,
shroud the sun.

The wilderness
stretches wide
and far,
fields flung
frozen
forever.

Blanketed,
clutching this fist full of faith,
I've thrown my arms around your neck,
burrowed my face in your mane,
to trust the cadence
of your steady intention,
to ride the rhythm
of your determined heart, and yes,
to sense the simplification
of a life unsnarled.

I can feel a gradual letting go,
the dissolution
of my delusions.

Be my compass.
Be my momentum.

I will lean into the horizon
and ride down the miles
'til I find myself

home.

scripture passages for sojourners

Psalm 40:1-5

I waited patiently for the Lord;
And He inclined to me,
And heard my cry.
He also brought me up out of a horrible pit,
Out of the miry clay,
And set my feet upon a rock,
And established my steps.

He has put a new song in my mouth—
Praise to our God;
Many will see it and fear,
And will trust in the Lord.
Blessed is that man who makes the Lord his trust,
And does not respect the proud,
Nor such as turn aside to lies.

Many, O Lord my God, are Your wonderful works
Which You have done;
And Your thoughts toward us
Cannot be recounted to You in order;
If I would declare and speak of them,
They are more than can be numbered.

Psalm 34:1-12

I will bless the Lord at all times;

His praise shall continually be in my mouth.

My soul shall make its boast in the Lord;

The humble shall hear of it and be glad.

Oh, magnify the Lord with me,

And let us exalt His name together.

I sought the Lord, and He heard me,

And delivered me from all my fears.

They looked to Him and were radiant,

And their faces were not ashamed.

This poor man cried out, and the Lord heard him,

And saved him out of all his troubles.

The angel of the Lord

encamps all around those who fear Him,

And delivers them.

Oh, taste and see that the Lord is good;

Blessed is the man who trusts in Him!

Oh, fear the Lord, you His saints!

There is no want to those who fear Him.

The young lions lack and suffer hunger;

But those who seek the Lord shall not lack any good thing.

Come, you children, listen to me;
I will teach you the fear of the Lord.
Who is the man who desires life,
And loves many days, that he may see good?
Keep your tongue from evil,
And your lips from speaking deceit.
Depart from evil and do good;
Seek peace and pursue it.

Matthew 5:3-10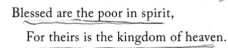

Blessed are the poor in spirit,

    For theirs is the kingdom of heaven.

Blessed are those who mourn,

    For they shall be comforted.

Blessed are the meek,

    For they shall inherit the earth.

Blessed are those who hunger and thirst for righteousness,

    For they shall be filled.

Blessed are the merciful,

    For they shall obtain mercy.

Blessed are the pure in heart,

    For they shall see God.

Blessed are the peacemakers,

    For they shall be called sons of God.

Blessed are those who are persecuted for righteousness' sake,

    For theirs is the kingdom of heaven.

Blessed for all.

Psalm 139:1-12

Lord, You have searched me and known me.

You know my sitting down and my rising up;

You understand my thought afar off.

You comprehend my path and my lying down,

And are acquainted with all my ways.

For there is not a word on my tongue,

But behold, O Lord, You know it altogether.

You have hedged me behind and before,

And laid Your hand upon me.

Such knowledge is too wonderful for me;

It is high, I cannot attain it.

Where can I go from Your Spirit?

Or where can I flee from Your presence?

If I ascend into heaven, You are there;

If I make my bed in hell, behold, You are there.

If I take the wings of the morning,

And dwell in the uttermost parts of the sea,

Even there Your hand shall lead me,

And Your right hand shall hold me.

If I say, "Surely the darkness shall fall on me,"

Even the night shall be light about me;

Indeed, the darkness shall not hide from You,

But the night shines as the day;
The darkness and the light are both alike to You.

Isaiah 41:17-20

The poor and needy seek water, but there is none,

Their tongues fail for thirst.

I, the Lord, will hear them;

I, the God of Israel, will not forsake them.

I will open rivers in desolate heights,

And fountains in the midst of the valleys;

I will make the wilderness a pool of water,

And the dry land springs of water.

I will plant in the wilderness the cedar and the acacia tree,

The myrtle and the oil tree;

I will set in the desert the cypress tree and the pine

And the box tree together,

That they may see and know,

And consider and understand together,

That the hand of the Lord has done this,

And the Holy One of Israel has created it.

Jeremiah 12:5

If you have run with the footmen, and they have wearied you,
Then how can you contend with horses?
And if in the land of peace,
In which you trusted, they wearied you,
Then how will you do in the floodplain of the Jordan?

Psalm 42

As the deer pants for the water brooks,
So pants my soul for You, O God.
My soul thirsts for God, for the living God.
When shall I come and appear before God?
My tears have been my food day and night,
While they continually say to me,
"Where is your God?"

When I remember these things,
I pour out my soul within me.
For I used to go with the multitude;
I went with them to the house of God,
With the voice of joy and praise,
With a multitude that kept a pilgrim feast.

Why are you cast down, O my soul?
And why are you disquieted within me?
Hope in God, for I shall yet praise Him
For the help of His countenance.

O my God, my soul is cast down within me;
Therefore I will remember You from the land of the Jordan,
And from the heights of Hermon,

From the Hill Mizar.

Deep calls unto deep at the noise of Your waterfalls;

All Your waves and billows have gone over me.

The Lord will command His lovingkindness in the daytime,

And in the night His song shall be with me—

A prayer to the God of my life.

I will say to God my Rock,

"Why have You forgotten me?

Why do I go mourning because of the oppression

of the enemy?"

As with a breaking of my bones,

My enemies reproach me,

While they say to me all day long,

"Where is your God?"

Why are you cast down, O my soul?

And why are you disquieted within me?

Hope in God;

For I shall yet praise Him,

The help of my countenance and my God.

Psalm 139:13-24

For You formed my inward parts;

You covered me in my mother's womb.

I will praise You, for I am fearfully and wonderfully made;

Marvelous are Your works,

And that my soul knows very well.

My frame was not hidden from You,

When I was made in secret,

And skillfully wrought in the lowest parts of the earth.

Your eyes saw my substance, being yet unformed.

And in Your book they all were written,

The days fashioned for me,

When as yet there were none of them.

How precious also are Your thoughts to me, O God!

How great is the sum of them!

If I should count them, they would be more in number than the

sand;

When I awake, I am still with You.

Oh, that You would slay the wicked, O God!

Depart from me, therefore, you bloodthirsty men.

For they speak against You wickedly;

Your enemies take Your name in vain.

Do I not hate them, O Lord, who hate You?
And do I not loathe those who rise up against You?
I hate them with perfect hatred;
I count them my enemies.

Search me, O God, and know my heart;
Try me, and know my anxieties;
And see if there is any wicked way in me,
And lead me in the way everlasting.

Psalm 102

Hear my prayer, O Lord,
And let my cry come to You.
Do not hide Your face from me in the day of my trouble;
Incline Your ear to me;
In the day that I call, answer me speedily.

For my days are consumed like smoke,
And my bones are burned like a hearth.
My heart is stricken and withered like grass,
So that I forget to eat my bread.
Because of the sound of my groaning
My bones cling to my skin.
I am like a pelican of the wilderness;
I am like an owl of the desert.
I lie awake,
And am like a sparrow alone on the housetop.

My enemies reproach me all day long;
Those who deride me swear an oath against me.
For I have eaten ashes like bread,
And mingled my drink with weeping,
Because of Your indignation and Your wrath;
For You have lifted me up and cast me away.

My days are like a shadow that lengthens,
And I wither away like grass.

But You, O Lord, shall endure forever,
And the remembrance of Your name to all generations.
You will arise and have mercy on Zion;
For the time to favor her,
Yes, the set time, has come.
For Your servants take pleasure in her stones,
And show favor to her dust.
So the nations shall fear the name of the Lord,
And all the kings of the earth Your glory.
For the Lord shall build up Zion;
He shall appear in His glory.
He shall regard the prayer of the destitute,
And shall not despise their prayer.

This will be written for the generation to come,
That a people yet to be created may praise the Lord.
For He looked down from the height of His sanctuary;
From heaven the Lord viewed the earth,
To hear the groaning of the prisoner,
To release those appointed to death,
To declare the name of the Lord in Zion,
And His praise in Jerusalem,

When the peoples are gathered together,
And the kingdoms, to serve the Lord.

He weakened my strength in the way;
He shortened my days.
I said, "O my God,
Do not take me away in the midst of my days;
Your years are throughout all generations.
Of old You laid the foundation of the earth,
And the heavens are the work of Your hands.
They will perish, but You will endure;
Yes, they will all grow old like a garment;
Like a cloak You will change them,
And they will be changed.
But You are the same,
And Your years will have no end.
The children of Your servants will continue,
And their descendants will be established before You."

Psalm 51:15-19

O Lord, open my lips,

And my mouth shall show forth Your praise.

For You do not desire sacrifice, or else I would give it;

You do not delight in burnt offering.

The sacrifices of God are a broken spirit,

A broken and a contrite heart—

These, O God, You will not despise.

Do good in Your good pleasure to Zion;

Build the walls of Jerusalem.

Then You shall be pleased with the sacrifices of righteousness,

With burnt offering and whole burnt offering;

Then they shall offer bulls on Your altar.

Isaiah 50:10-11

Who among you fears the Lord?
Who obeys the voice of His Servant?
Who walks in darkness
And has no light?
Let him trust in the name of the Lord
And rely upon his God.
Look, all you who kindle a fire,
Who encircle yourselves with sparks:
Walk in the light of your fire
and in the sparks you have kindled—
This you shall have from My hand:
You shall lie down in torment.

Psalm 69

Save me, O God!

For the waters have come up to my neck.

I sink in deep mire,

Where there is no standing;

I have come into deep waters,

Where the floods overflow me.

I am weary with my crying;

My throat is dry;

My eyes fail while I wait for my God.

Those who hate me without a cause

Are more than the hairs of my head;

They are mighty who would destroy me,

Being my enemies wrongfully;

Though I have stolen nothing,

I still must restore it.

O God, You know my foolishness;

And my sins are not hidden from You.

Let not those who wait for You,

O Lord GOD of hosts, be ashamed because of me;

Let not those who seek You be confounded because of me,

O God of Israel.

Because for Your sake I have borne reproach;
Shame has covered my face.
I have become a stranger to my brothers,
And an alien to my mother's children;
Because zeal for Your house has eaten me up,
And the reproaches of those who reproach
You have fallen on me.
When I wept and chastened my soul with fasting,
That became my reproach.
I also made sackcloth my garment;
I became a byword to them.
Those who sit in the gate speak against me,
And I am the song of the drunkards.

But as for me, my prayer is to You,
O Lord, in the acceptable time;
O God, in the multitude of Your mercy,
Hear me in the truth of Your salvation.
Deliver me out of the mire,
And let me not sink;
Let me be delivered from those who hate me,
And out of the deep waters.
Let not the floodwater overflow me,
Nor let the deep swallow me up;
And let not the pit shut its mouth on me.

Hear me, O Lord, for Your lovingkindness is good;
Turn to me according to the multitude of Your tender mercies.
And do not hide Your face from Your servant,
For I am in trouble;
Hear me speedily.
Draw near to my soul, and redeem it;
Deliver me because of my enemies.

You know my reproach, my shame, and my dishonor;
My adversaries are all before You.
Reproach has broken my heart,
And I am full of heaviness;
I looked for someone to take pity, but there was none;
And for comforters, but I found none.
They also gave me gall for my food,
And for my thirst they gave me vinegar to drink.

Let their table become a snare before them,
And their well-being a trap.
Let their eyes be darkened, so that they do not see;
And make their loins shake continually.
Pour out Your indignation upon them,
And let Your wrathful anger take hold of them.
Let their dwelling place be desolate;
Let no one live in their tents.

For they persecute the ones You have struck,
And talk of the grief of those You have wounded.
Add iniquity to their iniquity,
And let them not come into Your righteousness.
Let them be blotted out of the book of the living,
And not be written with the righteous.

But I am poor and sorrowful;
Let Your salvation, O God, set me up on high.
I will praise the name of God with a song,
And will magnify Him with thanksgiving.
This also shall please the Lord better than an ox or bull,
Which has horns and hooves.
The humble shall see this and be glad;
And you who seek God, your hearts shall live.

For the Lord hears the poor,
And does not despise His prisoners.
Let heaven and earth praise Him,
The seas and everything that moves in them.
For God will save Zion
And build the cities of Judah,
That they may dwell there and possess it.
Also, the descendants of His servants shall inherit it,
And those who love His name shall dwell in it.

Isaiah 38:11-20

I said,

"I shall not see Yah,

The Lord in the land of the living;

I shall observe man no more

among the inhabitants of the world.

My life span is gone,

Taken from me like a shepherd's tent;

I have cut off my life like a weaver.

He cuts me off from the loom;

From day until night You make an end of me.

I have considered until morning—

Like a lion,

So He breaks all my bones;

From day until night You make an end of me.

Like a crane or a swallow, so I chattered;

I mourned like a dove;

My eyes fail from looking upward.

O Lord, I am oppressed;

Undertake for me!

"What shall I say?

He has both spoken to me,

And He Himself has done it.

I shall walk carefully all my years

In the bitterness of my soul.

O Lord, by these things men live;

And in all these things is the life of my spirit;

So You will restore me and make me live.

Indeed it was for my own peace

That I had great bitterness;

But You have lovingly delivered my soul

from the pit of corruption,

For You have cast all my sins behind Your back.

For Sheol cannot thank You,

Death cannot praise You;

Those who go down to the pit cannot hope for Your truth.

The living, the living man, he shall praise You,

As I do this day;

The father shall make known Your truth to the children.

"The Lord was ready to save me;

Therefore we will sing my songs with stringed instruments

All the days of our life, in the house of the Lord."

Psalm 118:24

This is the day the Lord has made;
We will rejoice and be glad in it.

Psalm 23

The Lord is my shepherd;
I shall not want.
He makes me to lie down in green pastures;
He leads me beside the still waters.
He restores my soul;
He leads me in the paths of righteousness
For His name's sake.

Yea, though I walk through the valley of the shadow of death,
I will fear no evil;
For You are with me;
Your rod and Your staff, they comfort me.

You prepare a table before me in the presence of my enemies;
You anoint my head with oil;
My cup runs over.
Surely goodness and mercy shall follow me
All the days of my life;
And I will dwell in the house of the Lord
Forever.

I Samuel 2:1-9

And Hannah prayed and said:

My heart rejoices in the Lord;
My horn is exalted in the Lord.
I smile at my enemies,
Because I rejoice in Your salvation.

No one is holy like the Lord,
For there is none besides You,
Nor is there any rock like our God.

Talk no more so very proudly;
Let no arrogance come from your mouth,
For the Lord is the God of knowledge;
And by Him actions are weighed.

The bows of the mighty men are broken,
And those who stumbled are girded with strength.
Those who were full have hired themselves out for bread,
And the hungry have ceased to hunger.
Even the barren has borne seven,
And she who has many children has become feeble.
The Lord kills and makes alive;

He brings down to the grave and brings up.

The Lord makes poor and makes rich;

He brings low and lifts up.

He raises the poor from the dust

And lifts the beggar from the ash heap,

To set them among princes

And make them inherit the throne of glory.

For the pillars of the earth are the Lord's,

And He has set the world upon them.

He will guard the feet of His saints,

But the wicked shall be silent in darkness.

For by strength no man shall prevail.

Isaiah 55

"Ho! Everyone who thirsts,

Come to the waters;

And you who have no money,

Come, buy and eat.

Yes, come, buy wine and milk

Without money and without price.

Why do you spend money for what is not bread,

And your wages for what does not satisfy?

Listen carefully to Me, and eat what is good,

And let your soul delight itself in abundance.

Incline your ear, and come to Me.

Hear, and your soul shall live;

And I will make an everlasting covenant with you—

The sure mercies of David.

Indeed I have given him as a witness to the people,

A leader and commander for the people.

Surely you shall call a nation you do not know,

And nations who do not know you shall run to you,

Because of the Lord your God,

And the Holy One of Israel;

For He has glorified you."

Seek the Lord while He may be found,

Call upon Him while He is near.
Let the wicked forsake his way,
And the unrighteous man his thoughts;
Let him return to the Lord,
And He will have mercy on him;
And to our God,
For He will abundantly pardon.

"For My thoughts are not your thoughts,
Nor are your ways My ways," says the Lord.
"For as the heavens are higher than the earth,
So are My ways higher than your ways,
And My thoughts than your thoughts.

"For as the rain comes down, and the snow from heaven,
And do not return there,
But water the earth,
And make it bring forth and bud,
That it may give seed to the sower
And bread to the eater,
So shall My word be that goes forth from My mouth;
It shall not return to Me void,
But it shall accomplish what I please,
And it shall prosper in the thing for which I sent it.

"For you shall go out with joy,

And be led out with peace;

The mountains and the hills

Shall break forth into singing before you,

And all the trees of the field shall clap their hands.

Instead of the thorn shall come up the cypress tree,

And instead of the brier shall come up the myrtle tree;

And it shall be to the Lord for a name,

For an everlasting sign that shall not be cut off."

Isaiah 42:14-16

"I have held My peace a long time,
I have been still and restrained Myself.
Now I will cry like a woman in labor,
I will pant and gasp at once.
I will lay waste the mountains and hills,
And dry up all their vegetation;
I will make the rivers coastlands,
And I will dry up the pools.

I will bring the blind by a way they did not know;
I will lead them in paths they have not known.
I will make darkness light before them,
And crooked places straight.
These things I will do for them,
And not forsake them.

Psalm 103

Bless the Lord, O my soul;

And all that is within me, bless His holy name!

Bless the Lord, O my soul,

And forget not all His benefits:

Who forgives all your iniquities,

Who heals all your diseases,

Who redeems your life from destruction,

Who crowns you with lovingkindness and tender mercies,

Who satisfies your mouth with good things,

So that your youth is renewed like the eagle's.

The Lord executes righteousness

And justice for all who are oppressed.

He made known His ways to Moses,

His acts to the children of Israel.

The Lord is merciful and gracious,

Slow to anger, and abounding in mercy.

He will not always strive with us,

Nor will He keep His anger forever.

He has not dealt with us according to our sins,

Nor punished us according to our iniquities.

For as the heavens are high above the earth,

So great is His mercy toward those who fear Him;

As far as the east is from the west,

So far has He removed our transgressions from us.

As a father pities his children,

So the Lord pities those who fear Him.

For He knows our frame;

He remembers that we are dust.

As for man, his days are like grass;

As a flower of the field, so he flourishes.

For the wind passes over it, and it is gone,

And its place remembers it no more.

But the mercy of the Lord is from everlasting to everlasting

On those who fear Him,

And His righteousness to children's children,

To such as keep His covenant,

And to those who remember His commandments to do them.

The Lord has established His throne in heaven,

And His kingdom rules over all.

Bless the Lord, you His angels,

Who excel in strength, who do His word,

Heeding the voice of His word.

Bless the Lord, all you His hosts,

You ministers of His, who do His pleasure.

Bless the Lord, all His works,

In all places of His dominion.

Bless the Lord, O my soul!

Numbers 11:4-6

Now the mixed multitude who were among them yielded to intense craving; so the children of Israel also wept again and said: "Who will give us meat to eat? We remember the fish which we ate freely in Egypt, the cucumbers, the melons, the leeks, the onions, and the garlic; but now our whole being is dried up; there is nothing at all except this manna before our eyes!"

Joel 2:21-27

Fear not, O land;

Be glad and rejoice,

For the Lord has done marvelous things!

Do not be afraid, you beasts of the field;

For the open pastures are springing up,

And the tree bears its fruit;

The fig tree and the vine yield their strength.

Be glad then, you children of Zion,

And rejoice in the Lord your God;

For He has given you the former rain faithfully,

And He will cause the rain to come down for you—

The former rain,

And the latter rain in the first month.

The threshing floors shall be full of wheat,

And the vats shall overflow with new wine and oil.

"So I will restore to you the years that the swarming locust

has eaten,

The crawling locust,

The consuming locust,

And the chewing locust,

My great army which I sent among you.

You shall eat in plenty and be satisfied,

And praise the name of the Lord your God,

Who has dealt wondrously with you;

And My people shall never be put to shame.

Then you shall know that I am in the midst of Israel:

I am the Lord your God

And there is no other.

My people shall never be put to shame.

Psalm 130

Out of the depths I have cried to You, O Lord;
Lord, hear my voice!
Let Your ears be attentive
To the voice of my supplications.

If You, Lord, should mark iniquities,
O Lord, who could stand?
But there is forgiveness with You,
That You may be feared.

I wait for the Lord, my soul waits,
And in His word I do hope.
My soul waits for the Lord
More than those who watch for the morning—
Yes, more than those who watch for the morning.

O Israel, hope in the Lord;
For with the Lord there is mercy,
And with Him is abundant redemption.
And He shall redeem Israel
From all his iniquities.

Matthew 6:25-32

"Therefore I say to you, do not worry about your life, what you will eat or what you will drink; nor about your body, what you will put on. Is not life more than food and the body more than clothing? Look at the birds of the air, for they neither sow nor reap nor gather into barns; yet your heavenly Father feeds them. Are you not of more value than they? Which of you by worrying can add one cubit to his stature?

"So why do you worry about clothing? Consider the lilies of the field, how they grow: they neither toil nor spin; and yet I say to you that even Solomon in all his glory was not arrayed like one of these. Now if God so clothes the grass of the field, which today is, and tomorrow is thrown into the oven, will He not much more clothe you, O you of little faith?

"Therefore do not worry, saying, 'What shall we eat?' or 'What shall we drink?' or 'What shall we wear?' For after all these things the Gentiles seek. For your heavenly Father knows that you need all these things."

Psalm 71

God is with you and in Love with you!

In You, O Lord, I put my trust;

Let me never be put to shame.

Deliver me in Your righteousness, and cause me to escape;

Incline Your ear to me, and save me.

Be my strong refuge,

To which I may resort continually;

You have given the commandment to save me,

For You are my rock and my fortress.

Deliver me, O my God, out of the hand of the wicked,

Out of the hand of the unrighteous and cruel man.

For You are my hope, O Lord GOD;

You are my trust from my youth.

By You I have been upheld from birth;

You are He who took me out of my mother's womb.

My praise shall be continually of You.

I have become as a wonder to many,

But You are my strong refuge.

Let my mouth be filled with Your praise

And with Your glory all the day.

Do not cast me off in the time of old age;

Do not forsake me when my strength fails.

191

For my enemies speak against me;

And those who lie in wait for my life take counsel together,

Saying, "God has forsaken him;

Pursue and take him, for there is none to deliver him."

O God, do not be far from me;

O my God, make haste to help me!

Let them be confounded and consumed

Who are adversaries of my life;

Let them be covered with reproach and dishonor

Who seek my hurt.

But I will hope continually,

And will praise You yet more and more.

My mouth shall tell of Your righteousness

And Your salvation all the day,

For I do not know their limits.

I will go in the strength of the Lord GOD;

I will make mention of Your righteousness, of Yours only.

O God, You have taught me from my youth;

And to this day I declare Your wondrous works.

Now also when I am old and grayheaded,

O God, do not forsake me,

Until I declare Your strength to this generation,

Your power to everyone who is to come.

Also Your righteousness, O God, is very high,
You who have done great things;
O God, who is like You?
You, who have shown me great and severe troubles,
Shall revive me again,
And bring me up again from the depths of the earth.
You shall increase my greatness,
And comfort me on every side.

Also with the lute I will praise You—
And Your faithfulness, O my God!
To You I will sing with the harp,
O Holy One of Israel.
My lips shall greatly rejoice when I sing to You,
And my soul, which You have redeemed.
My tongue also shall talk of Your righteousness all the day long;
For they are confounded,
For they are brought to shame
Who seek my hurt.

Psalm 20

May the Lord answer you in the day of trouble;
May the name of the God of Jacob defend you;
May He send you help from the sanctuary,
And strengthen you out of Zion;
May He remember all your offerings,
And accept your burnt sacrifice. Selah

May He grant you according to your heart's desire,
And fulfill all your purpose.
We will rejoice in your salvation,
And in the name of our God we will set up our banners!
May the Lord fulfill all your petitions.

Now I know that the Lord saves His anointed;
He will answer him from His holy heaven
With the saving strength of His right hand.

Some trust in chariots, and some in horses;
But we will remember the name of the Lord our God.
They have bowed down and fallen;
But we have risen and stand upright.

Save, Lord! May the King answer us when we call.

Isaiah 63

Who is this who comes from Edom,
With dyed garments from Bozrah,
This One who is glorious in His apparel,
Traveling in the greatness of His strength?—

"I who speak in righteousness, mighty to save."

Why is Your apparel red,
And Your garments like one who treads in the winepress?

"I have trodden the winepress alone,
And from the peoples no one was with Me.
For I have trodden them in My anger,
And trampled them in My fury;
Their blood is sprinkled upon My garments,
And I have stained all My robes.
For the day of vengeance is in My heart,
And the year of My redeemed has come.
I looked, but there was no one to help,
And I wondered
That there was no one to uphold;
Therefore My own arm brought salvation for Me;
And My own fury, it sustained Me.

I have trodden down the peoples in My anger,
Made them drunk in My fury,
And brought down their strength to the earth."

I will mention the lovingkindnesses of the Lord
And the praises of the Lord,
According to all that the Lord has bestowed on us,
And the great goodness toward the house of Israel,
Which He has bestowed on them according to His mercies,
According to the multitude of His lovingkindnesses.
For He said, "Surely they are My people,
Children who will not lie."
So He became their Savior.
In all their affliction He was afflicted,
And the Angel of His Presence saved them;
In His love and in His pity He redeemed them;
And He bore them and carried them
All the days of old.
But they rebelled and grieved His Holy Spirit;
So He turned Himself against them as an enemy,
And He fought against them.

Then he remembered the days of old,
Moses and his people, saying:
"Where is He who brought them up out of the sea
With the shepherd of His flock?

Where is He who put His Holy Spirit within them,
Who led them by the right hand of Moses,
With His glorious arm,
Dividing the water before them
To make for Himself an everlasting name,
Who led them through the deep,
As a horse in the wilderness,
That they might not stumble?"

As a beast goes down into the valley,
And the Spirit of the Lord causes him to rest,
So You lead Your people,
To make Yourself a glorious name.
A Prayer of Penitence

Look down from heaven,
And see from Your habitation, holy and glorious.
Where are Your zeal and Your strength,
The yearning of Your heart and Your mercies toward me?
Are they restrained?
Doubtless You are our Father,
Though Abraham was ignorant of us,
And Israel does not acknowledge us.
You, O Lord, are our Father;
Our Redeemer from Everlasting is Your name.
O Lord, why have You made us stray from Your ways,

And hardened our heart from Your fear?

Return for Your servants' sake,

The tribes of Your inheritance.

Your holy people have possessed it but a little while;

Our adversaries have trodden down Your sanctuary.

We have become like those of old, over whom You never ruled,

Those who were never called by Your name.

Jeremiah 29:10-14

For thus says the Lord: After seventy years are completed at Babylon, I will visit you and perform My good word toward you, and cause you to return to this place. For I know the thoughts that I think toward you, says the Lord, thoughts of peace and not of evil, to give you a future and a hope.

Then you will call upon Me and go and pray to Me, and I will listen to you. And you will seek Me and find Me, when you search for Me with all your heart. I will be found by you, says the Lord, and I will bring you back from your captivity; I will gather you from all the nations and from all the places where I have driven you, says the Lord, and I will bring you to the place from which I cause you to be carried away captive.

Psalm 40

I waited patiently for the Lord;
And He inclined to me,
And heard my cry.
He also brought me up out of a horrible pit,
Out of the miry clay,
And set my feet upon a rock,
And established my steps.
He has put a new song in my mouth—
Praise to our God;
Many will see it and fear,
And will trust in the Lord.

Blessed is that man who makes the Lord his trust,
And does not respect the proud, nor such as turn aside
to lies.
Many, O Lord my God, are Your wonderful works
Which You have done;
And Your thoughts toward us
Cannot be recounted to You in order;
If I would declare and speak of them,
They are more than can be numbered.

Sacrifice and offering You did not desire;

My ears You have opened.

Burnt offering and sin offering You did not require.

Then I said, "Behold, I come;

In the scroll of the book it is written of me.

I delight to do Your will, O my God,

And Your law is within my heart."

I have proclaimed the good news of righteousness

In the great assembly;

Indeed, I do not restrain my lips,

O Lord, You Yourself know.

I have not hidden Your righteousness within my heart;

I have declared Your faithfulness and Your salvation;

I have not concealed Your lovingkindness and Your truth

From the great assembly.

Do not withhold Your tender mercies from me, O Lord;

Let Your lovingkindness and Your truth continually preserve me.

For innumerable evils have surrounded me;

My iniquities have overtaken me, so that I am not able to look up;

They are more than the hairs of my head;

Therefore my heart fails me.

Be pleased, O Lord, to deliver me;

O Lord, make haste to help me!

Let them be ashamed and brought to mutual confusion
Who seek to destroy my life;
Let them be driven backward and brought to dishonor
Who wish me evil.
Let them be confounded because of their shame,
Who say to me, "Aha, aha!"

Let all those who seek You rejoice and be glad in You;
Let such as love Your salvation say continually,
"The Lord be magnified!"
But I am poor and needy;
Yet the Lord thinks upon me.
You are my help and my deliverer;
Do not delay, O my God.

Isaiah 30:15-25

For thus says the Lord God, the Holy One of Israel:

"In returning and rest you shall be saved;
In quietness and confidence shall be your strength."
But you would not,
And you said, "No, for we will flee on horses"—
Therefore you shall flee!
And, "We will ride on swift horses"—
Therefore those who pursue you shall be swift!

One thousand shall flee at the threat of one,
At the threat of five you shall flee,
Till you are left as a pole on top of a mountain
And as a banner on a hill.

Therefore the Lord will wait, that He may be gracious
to you;
And therefore He will be exalted, that He may have
mercy on you.

For the Lord is a God of justice;
Blessed are all those who wait for Him.
For the people shall dwell in Zion at Jerusalem;

You shall weep no more.

He will be very gracious to you at the sound of your cry;

When He hears it, He will answer you.

And though the Lord gives you

The bread of adversity and the water of affliction,

Yet your teachers will not be moved into a corner anymore,

But your eyes shall see your teachers.

Lamentations 3:1-24

I am the man who has seen affliction by the rod of
His wrath.
He has led me and made me walk
In darkness and not in light.
Surely He has turned His hand against me
Time and time again throughout the day.

He has aged my flesh and my skin,
And broken my bones.
He has besieged me
And surrounded me with bitterness and woe.
He has set me in dark places
Like the dead of long ago.

He has hedged me in so that I cannot get out;
He has made my chain heavy.
Even when I cry and shout,
He shuts out my prayer.
He has blocked my ways with hewn stone;
He has made my paths crooked.

He has been to me a bear lying in wait,
Like a lion in ambush.

He has turned aside my ways and torn me in pieces;
He has made me desolate.
He has bent His bow
And set me up as a target for the arrow.

He has caused the arrows of His quiver
To pierce my loins.
I have become the ridicule of all my people—
Their taunting song all the day.
He has filled me with bitterness,
He has made me drink wormwood.

He has also broken my teeth with gravel,
And covered me with ashes.
You have moved my soul far from peace;
I have forgotten prosperity.
And I said, "My strength and my hope
Have perished from the Lord."

Remember my affliction and roaming,
The wormwood and the gall.
My soul still remembers
And sinks within me.
This I recall to my mind,
Therefore I have hope.

Through the Lord's mercies we are not consumed,
Because His compassions fail not.
They are new every morning;
Great is Your faithfulness.
"The Lord is my portion," says my soul,
"Therefore I hope in Him!"

Psalm 6

O Lord, do not rebuke me in Your anger,
Nor chasten me in Your hot displeasure.
Have mercy on me, O Lord, for I am weak;
O Lord, heal me, for my bones are troubled.
My soul also is greatly troubled;
But You, O Lord—how long?
Return, O Lord, deliver me!
Oh, save me for Your mercies' sake!
For in death there is no remembrance of You;
In the grave who will give You thanks?

I am weary with my groaning;
All night I make my bed swim;
I drench my couch with my tears.
My eye wastes away because of grief;
It grows old because of all my enemies.

Depart from me, all you workers of iniquity;
For the Lord has heard the voice of my weeping.
The Lord has heard my supplication;
The Lord will receive my prayer.
Let all my enemies be ashamed and greatly troubled;
Let them turn back and be ashamed suddenly.

Habakkuk 3:17-19

Though the fig tree may not blossom,
Nor fruit be on the vines;
Though the labor of the olive may fail,
And the fields yield no food;
Though the flock may be cut off from the fold,
And there be no herd in the stalls—
Yet I will rejoice in the Lord,
I will joy in the God of my salvation.

The Lord God is my strength;
He will make my feet like deer's feet,
And He will make me walk on my high hills.

Psalm 114

When Israel went out of Egypt,
The house of Jacob from a people of strange language,
Judah became His sanctuary,
And Israel His dominion.

The sea saw it and fled;
Jordan turned back.
The mountains skipped like rams,
The little hills like lambs.
What ails you, O sea, that you fled?
O Jordan, that you turned back?
O mountains, that you skipped like rams?
O little hills, like lambs?

Tremble, O earth, at the presence of the Lord,
At the presence of the God of Jacob,
Who turned the rock into a pool of water,
The flint into a fountain of waters.

Psalm 19:1-11

The heavens declare the glory of God;
And the firmament shows His handiwork.
Day unto day utters speech,
And night unto night reveals knowledge.
There is no speech nor language
Where their voice is not heard.
Their line has gone out through all the earth,
And their words to the end of the world.

In them He has set a tabernacle for the sun,
Which is like a bridegroom coming out of his chamber,
And rejoices like a strong man to run its race.
Its rising is from one end of heaven,
And its circuit to the other end;
And there is nothing hidden from its heat.

The law of the Lord is perfect, converting the soul;
The testimony of the Lord is sure, making wise the
simple;
The statutes of the Lord are right, rejoicing the heart;
The commandment of the Lord is pure, enlightening the
eyes;

The fear of the Lord is clean, enduring forever;

The judgments of the Lord are true and righteous altogether.

More to be desired are they than gold,

Yea, than much fine gold;

Sweeter also than honey and the honeycomb.

Moreover by them Your servant is warned,

And in keeping them there is great reward.

Psalm 51:1-13

Have mercy upon me, O God,
According to Your lovingkindness;
According to the multitude of Your tender mercies,
Blot out my transgressions.
Wash me thoroughly from my iniquity,
And cleanse me from my sin.

For I acknowledge my transgressions,
And my sin is always before me.
Against You, You only, have I sinned,
And done this evil in Your sight—
That You may be found just when You speak,
And blameless when You judge.

Behold, I was brought forth in iniquity,
And in sin my mother conceived me.
Behold, You desire truth in the inward parts,
And in the hidden part You will make me to know wisdom.

Purge me with hyssop, and I shall be clean;
Wash me, and I shall be whiter than snow.
Make me hear joy and gladness,
That the bones You have broken may rejoice.

Hide Your face from my sins,
And blot out all my iniquities.

Create in me a clean heart, O God,
And renew a steadfast spirit within me.
Do not cast me away from Your presence,
And do not take Your Holy Spirit from me.

Restore to me the joy of Your salvation,
And uphold me by Your generous Spirit.
Then I will teach transgressors Your ways,
And sinners shall be converted to You.

Hosea 14:1-9

O Israel, return to the Lord your God,

For you have stumbled because of your iniquity;

Take words with you,

And return to the Lord.

Say to Him,

"Take away all iniquity;

Receive us graciously,

For we will offer the sacrifices of our lips.

Assyria shall not save us,

We will not ride on horses,

Nor will we say anymore to the work of our hands,

'You are our gods.'

For in You the fatherless finds mercy."

"I will heal their backsliding,

I will love them freely,

For My anger has turned away from him.

I will be like the dew to Israel;

He shall grow like the lily,

And lengthen his roots like Lebanon.

His branches shall spread;

His beauty shall be like an olive tree,

And his fragrance like Lebanon.

Those who dwell under his shadow shall return;
They shall be revived like grain,
And grow like a vine.
Their scent shall be like the wine of Lebanon.

"Ephraim shall say, 'What have I to do anymore with idols?'
I have heard and observed him.
I am like a green cypress tree;
Your fruit is found in Me."
Who is wise?
Let him understand these things.

Who is prudent?
Let him know them.
For the ways of the Lord are right;
The righteous walk in them,
But transgressors stumble in them.

Isaiah 40

Comfort, comfort my people,
    says your God.
Speak tenderly to Jerusalem,
    and proclaim to her
that her hard service has been completed,
    that her sin has been paid for,
that she has received from the Lord's hand
    double for all her sins.

A voice of one calling:
"In the wilderness prepare
    the way for the Lord;
make straight in the desert
    a highway for our God.
Every valley shall be raised up,
    every mountain and hill made low;
the rough ground shall become level,
    the rugged places a plain.
And the glory of the Lord will be revealed,
    and all people will see it together.
For the mouth of the Lord has spoken."

A voice says, "Cry out."

And I said, "What shall I cry?"
"All people are like grass,
   and all their faithfulness is like the flowers of the field.
The grass withers and the flowers fall,
   because the breath of the Lord blows on them.
   Surely the people are grass.
The grass withers and the flowers fall,
   but the word of our God endures forever."

You who bring good news to Zion,
   go up on a high mountain.
You who bring good news to Jerusalem,
   lift up your voice with a shout,
lift it up, do not be afraid;
   say to the towns of Judah,
   "Here is your God!"
See, the Sovereign Lord comes with power,
   and he rules with a mighty arm.
See, his reward is with him,
   and his recompense accompanies him.
He tends his flock like a shepherd:
   He gathers the lambs in his arms
and carries them close to his heart;
   he gently leads those that have young.

Who has measured the waters in the hollow of his hand,

or with the breadth of his hand marked off the heavens?
Who has held the dust of the earth in a basket,
    or weighed the mountains on the scales
    and the hills in a balance?
Who can fathom the Spirit of the Lord,
    or instruct the Lord as his counselor?
Whom did the Lord consult to enlighten him,
    and who taught him the right way?
Who was it that taught him knowledge,
    or showed him the path of understanding?
Surely the nations are like a drop in a bucket;
    they are regarded as dust on the scales;
    he weighs the islands as though they were fine dust.
Lebanon is not sufficient for altar fires,
    nor its animals enough for burnt offerings.
Before him all the nations are as nothing;
    they are regarded by him as worthless
    and less than nothing.

With whom, then, will you compare God?
    To what image will you liken him?
As for an idol, a metalworker casts it,
    and a goldsmith overlays it with gold
    and fashions silver chains for it.
A person too poor to present such an offering
    selects wood that will not rot;

they look for a skilled worker
    to set up an idol that will not topple.
Do you not know?
    Have you not heard?
Has it not been told you from the beginning?
    Have you not understood since the earth was founded?
He sits enthroned above the circle of the earth,
    and its people are like grasshoppers.
He stretches out the heavens like a canopy,
    and spreads them out like a tent to live in.
He brings princes to naught
    and reduces the rulers of this world to nothing.

No sooner are they planted,
    no sooner are they sown,
    no sooner do they take root in the ground,
than he blows on them and they wither,
    and a whirlwind sweeps them away like chaff.

"To whom will you compare me?
    Or who is my equal?" says the Holy One.
Lift up your eyes and look to the heavens:
    Who created all these?
He who brings out the starry host one by one
    and calls forth each of them by name.
Because of his great power and mighty strength,

not one of them is missing.

Why do you complain, Jacob?
   Why do you say, Israel,
"My way is hidden from the Lord;
   my cause is disregarded by my God"?
Do you not know?
   Have you not heard?
The Lord is the everlasting God,
   the Creator of the ends of the earth.
He will not grow tired or weary,
   and his understanding no one can fathom.
He gives strength to the weary
   and increases the power of the weak.
Even youths grow tired and weary,
   and young men stumble and fall;
but those who hope in the Lord
   will renew their strength.
They will soar on wings like eagles;
   they will run and not grow weary,
   they will walk and not be faint.

acknowledgments

Acknowledgments

Yes, this is a poem.
The last.
      For now.
The point at which
I point away
from me,
      finally,
to friends who said,
"Carry on!" or
"Stop!" or
"Why?" and
"What if?" and
to whom I owe
more than just a token gesture
of gratitude.

Dear friends
like Amy and Bill,
for example,
who willingly spent
part of their life
hunched over
my rough drafts,
untangling the fishing line

of my thoughts.

Or my parents,
who carried me when I was small
and who carry me still.

Or Eric,
one of those endangered species
who memorizes poems for fun
and who shares them
like a handful of gladness.

And, of course,
my wife and kids,
who are,
and always will be,
the harbor lights
guiding me home.

To these,
and those I've forgotten,
here's everything I truly have to offer:
my heart
and my gratefulness.

About the Author

Ben Palpant and his wife live in the Northwest with their five galloping children. He received his undergraduate degree from Whitworth University and teaches at The Oaks Classical and Christian Academy.

Find out what Ben Palpant is writing next and discover book trailers (and much more) at benpalpant.com

CPSIA information can be obtained
at www.ICGtesting.com
Printed in the USA
LVOW10s1744220617

539023LV00003B/669/P